In memory of Mary Upshaw Broach and for my

first grandchild, Kai Gray McGee, a very happy boy! ~ M M

For Freya ~ always say "boo" to a goose! ~ A E

Copyright © 2008 by Good Books, Intercourse, PA 17534
International Standard Book Number: 978-1-56148-615-1

Library of Congress Catalog Card Number: 2007032365

Text copyright © Marni McGee 2008
Illustrations copyright © Alison Edgson 2008

Original edition published in English by Little Tiger Press,
an imprint of Magi Publications, London, England, 2008.

Printed in Singapore

Library of Congress Cataloging-in-Publication Data

McGee, Marni.
Silly Goose / Marni McGee ; illustrated by Alison Edgson.
p. cm.

Summary: When Fox tricks Goose into believing she has lost her ears and needs a new pair,
Rabbit catches on and summons the other animals of Frog Jump Pond to help rescue her.
ISBN 978-1-56148-615-1 (hardcover)
[1. Geese--Fiction. 2. Foxes--Fiction. 3. Animals--Fiction. 4. Ear--Fiction. 5. Tricksters--Fiction.]
I. Edgson, Alison, ill. II. Title.

PZ7.M167515Sil 2008

[E]--dc22

2007032365

Silly
Goose

Marni McGee

illustrated by

Alison Edgson

Intercourse, PA 17534
800/762-7171
www.GoodBooks.com

Goose was very happy. Sun was shining. Bird was
singing. Bee was buzzing in the flowers. Goose began
to dance on the banks of Frog Jump Pond.

Goose saw Fox. "Good morning, Fox," she called.

But Fox didn't say, "Good morning." Instead he said,
"Goose, your ears are missing."

"My ears?" Goose
gasped. "Missing?"
    Fox held out
his paws. "Look
in the pond. What
do you see?"

Goose looked. "I see
my white feathers, my
long-long neck, and my beautiful wings."
  "Ah," said Fox, "but do you see your ears?"
  "Well no," said Goose, "but I can fix that, dear Fox."
And she set two pink flowers on her head.

"Pahhh," scoffed Fox. "Ears are not soft
and pink. Ears are stiff, pointy things—with fur."
"Where could my ears be?" wondered Goose.
"Did you take them off?" asked Fox.
"Must have," said Goose. "I guess . . .
May I have *your* ears, dear Fox?"

"No," snapped Fox, "you may not.
They are the wrong color for you."
    "Oh dear," said Goose. And
off she ran until she
met Rabbit.

"Rabbit," said Goose. "I have lost
my ears somewhere, somehow.
May I have *your* ears, dear Rabbit?"
"No, silly Goose," sighed Rabbit.
"They would be too long for you."
"Oh dear," said Goose, and off
she ran until she met Cow.

"Cow," cried Goose,
"I have lost my ears! I must,
I *must* have ears right now.
May I have *your* ears, dear Cow?"
"Such a silly Goose!" Cow grumbled.
"My ears would be too big for you."

"Oh dear, oh dear," wailed Goose.
But then she heard someone calling:

"Ears for sale!
Get your ears from Peacock's shop!"

Goose saw a
strange bird with
bright feathers, bows,
and trailing ribbons.

"I would like two white ears,
if you please," she said.
    Peacock bowed low. "Come to
my shop, Madam," he said. "We will
choose the perfect ears for a delicious—
I mean, *delightful*—creature like you."
  "Goodie," gushed Goose, and off they pranced.
    Goose did not notice his pointy snout,
his sharp teeth, or his bushy red tail.

But Rabbit saw. "Peacocks do *not* have pointy snouts, sharp teeth, or bushy red tails," he thought. His whiskers trembled with the truth: "Peacock is Fox in disguise!" Quickly he gathered the animals.

"Hurry-hurry-hurry," he cried.

"Fox has tricked our poor, silly Goose."

So the animals trotted, hopped,

and flew to save Goose.

Meanwhile Goose and Fox had reached his den.
"Stand near the fire, Goose," he commanded.
"I shall choose the perfect ears for you."

EARS
For
Sale

As she waited, Goose began to *think*. "I *hear* that
crackling fire, and I *heard* what Peacock said just now."
"Peacock," she exclaimed. "I can hear!"
"Pahhh," he scoffed. "You're imagining things."

Just then the animals arrived at Fox's den.
"Goose," called Rabbit, "are you there?"
"We have come," buzzed Bee.
"Are you there? Are you there?"

Goose flapped her wings with delight. "Peacock, I hear my friends. I *do not* need new ears. I have my ears . . . somewhere. I *am* a silly goose, I guess. And now I must be going. Goodbye, dear Peacock. Bye-bye."

"Oooooooh, no," Fox sneered and bolted
the door. "You are not going *anywhere*, Goose."
He flung off his cloak, his ribbons, and bows.
"Fox!" gasped Goose.
"Yes," said Fox. "It is I—Fox. And I am
going to eat you, Goose."
"Oh dear, oh DEAR," cried Goose.
"I am done-for, finished, COOKED!"

Just then, Bird pecked a hole in the wall—
big enough for Bee. Bee zoomed in
and stung Fox on the nose. Fox howled.
Goose honked with excitement.

With a flick of her wings, she snatched
Fox's cloak. She slung it over his head
and tied him up.

And then with one mighty kick,
Cow broke down the door.

Fox wriggled free and ran.
The animals ran after him.
With Goose in the lead, they chased
that wicked Fox far, far away...

With all of her friends around her—Rabbit, Cow, Bird, and Bee—Goose danced again on the banks of Frog Jump Pond.

Goose was very, very happy!